ABORIGINAL TECHNOLOGY

Boomerangs and Throwing Sticks

 ABORIGINAL TECHNOLOGY

Boomerangs and Throwing Sticks

Alex Barlow

Acknowledgements

The authors and publishers are grateful to the following for permission to reproduce copyright material.

Coo-ee Picture Library, cover, pp. 8, 10, 26, 27; Neil McLeod, pp. 10, 12, 13, 14, 17, 18, 22, 28; South Australian Museum, pp. 7, 11, 16, 19, 20, 21, 23.

While every care has been taken to trace and acknowledge copyright, the publishers tender their apologies for any accidental infringement where copyright has proved untraceable

Copyright © Alex Barlow 1994
Decorative borders © Elizabeth Djandilnga Thorne 1994
Illustrations pp. 6, 15, 24, 25 © Susie Parry 1994
Illustrations p. 9 © Xiangyi Mo

All rights reserved.
Except under the conditions described in the
Copyright Act 1968 of Australia and subsequent amendments,
no part of this publication may be reproduced,
stored in a retrieval system, or transmitted in any form or by any means,
electronic, mechanical, photocopying, recording or otherwise,
without the prior permission of the copyright owner.

First published 1994
This edition published 1998 by
MACMILLAN EDUCATION AUSTRALIA PTY LTD
627 Chapel Street, South Yarra 3141

Associated companies and representatives throughout the world.

National Library of Australia cataloguing in publication data.

Barlow, Alex.
    Boomerangs and throwing sticks.

    Includes index.
    ISBN 0 7329 5041 4.

    1. Aborigines, Australian – Implements – Juvenile literature.
    2. Boomerangs – Juvenile literature. 3. Throwing-sticks –
    Australia – Juvenile literature. I. Title.
    (Series: Barlow, Alex. Aboriginal technology).

623.441

Set in Palatino
Printed in Hong Kong

Contents

Making a throwing stick	6
A history of the throwing stick	8
Inventing the boomerang	11
Goose sticks	15
Clubs and throwing sticks	17
Returning boomerangs	23
Modern boomerangs	26
Glossary	29
Index	30

Making a throwing stick

See if you can find two flat sticks of equal length. Two old rulers would do. Tie them crossways at the centre, like this:

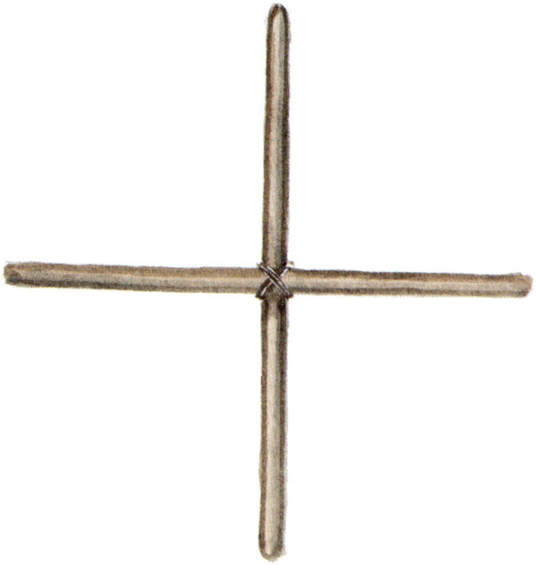

Take your sticks out into an open area where you can't hit anything or hurt anyone. Hold onto the end of one of the sticks and throw them up into the air in front of you. There, now you have made a type of throwing stick.

Early European settlers from around the Georges River in Sydney saw the Turuwal people throwing a curiously carved, angled stick that whirled around in the air and then returned to the thrower. They were told that it was a "bou-mar-ang." Nowadays, the word *boomerang* is the name we use for any kind of throwing stick that can be made to return to the thrower, no matter what shape it is or where it comes from. In other places, where throwing sticks were made by different groups of Aborigines, names such as *birgan*, *barragadan* and *wonguin* were used.

Throwing sticks are made in different shapes depending on how they are to be thrown and what purpose they are being used for.

A history of the throwing stick

Before the Europeans came to settle in Australia in 1788, nearly all of the original Australian people made and used throwing sticks. They were their most useful hunting tool and a dangerous weapon. Very few of them were designed to return to the thrower. Some people never made returning boomerangs since they were of little use for hunting. They were sometimes sent whirring over a flock of parrots feeding on the ground. Frightened by the sound and the shadow of the boomerang, the parrots would panic and fly wildly off the ground into the nets of the waiting hunters. This was not a common method of hunting and the number of small birds they caught this way didn't provide the hunters with much food.

This etching, drawn in 1850, depicts Aborigines on the Murray River using throwing sticks to kill birds.

The throwing sticks people commonly used came in a variety of different shapes and were used in different ways. Some throwing sticks could also be used as clubs. Others were little more than slightly curved sticks that ended in a point with a hand grip scratched into one end. Simple throwing sticks like these were mainly found in Tasmania and in parts of Western Australia. They had generally been replaced in southern and south-eastern Australia by more elaborately carved, curved throwing sticks and throwing clubs.

These simple throwing sticks come from different parts of the country:
a. Tasmania,
b. Western Australia,
c. Melville Island,
d. Western Australia,
e. Wardaman tribe, Northern Australia,
f. and g. Eastern Queensland.

This photo of an Aboriginal man throwing a boomerang and carrying a shield was taken in 1934.

There is plenty of evidence from around the world to show that Aborigines were not the only people to use carved pieces of wood as tools and weapons. Such evidence has come from southern India, Egypt, North Africa, the New Hebrides in the Pacific and the American Indians. We don't know a great deal about the design of the throwing sticks from these other countries, but we do know a lot about the designs used here in Australia.

Recent research on a large collection of throwing sticks found in the tomb of Tutankhamen in Egypt suggests that some of them were designed to return to the thrower. However, this does not rule out the claim that the development of the returning boomerang was an earlier and separate **invention** by Australia's Aboriginal people.

Inventing the boomerang

There is no way of knowing who invented the boomerang. The oldest boomerangs found in Australia lay in a **peat** bog (a kind of swamp) in South Australia for approximately 10 000 years. Normally objects made of wood do not last very long in the open air unless they are carefully preserved. Conditions in the bog helped to preserve twenty-five wooden tools including digging sticks, barbed spears and three complete boomerangs. Both the spears and the boomerangs are the oldest in the world. You can see these ancient wooden tools and weapons preserved in the South Australian museum.

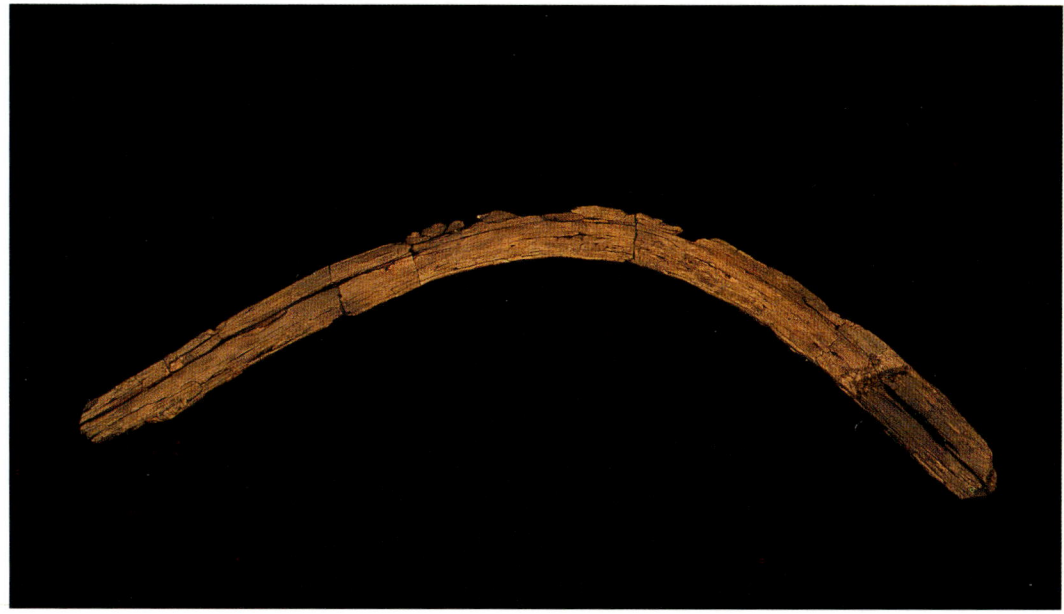

One of the ancient boomerangs found in Wyrie Swamp.

The main difference between returning boomerangs and throwing sticks is the way the sides and ends are shaped. The boomerangs found in Wyrie Swamp were shaped so that they would return to the thrower. Copies of these old boomerangs have been made and thrown.

These modern returning boomerangs come from Yalata in South Australia.

12

Can you guess how these wooden tools got into Wyrie Swamp? We can't know for certain of course, but around 10 000 years ago Aboriginal people probably lived beside the swamp, where they hunted, gathered food and made wooden tools. Stone tools were also found in Wyrie Swamp. These would have been used to make the wooden tools.

Why these particular boomerangs were left at the site to be found so many years later we cannot know. We can be grateful that they were left to be preserved in the swamp because they have revealed some very important information on how people lived in Australia thousands of years ago. I wonder what information will be available about how we live in Australia today in another 10 000 years time?

We have spoken so far about carved throwing sticks used for hunting. Throwing sticks were also used as ceremonial objects in religious rituals and as musical instruments. The designs of throwing sticks found throughout Australia varied according to what they were to be used for and what materials were available to carve them from. The best throwing sticks for hunting were those made of hard wood, which were heavy enough to seriously injure an animal and would not break on impact.

Hunters always tried to get as close as possible to the animal or whatever else they were hunting before throwing their sticks, spears or clubs at them. Important factors in choosing what type of throwing stick to use included how close they could get to the animal they were hunting, the size of the animal and the type of country they were in.

This man is making a boomerang.

13

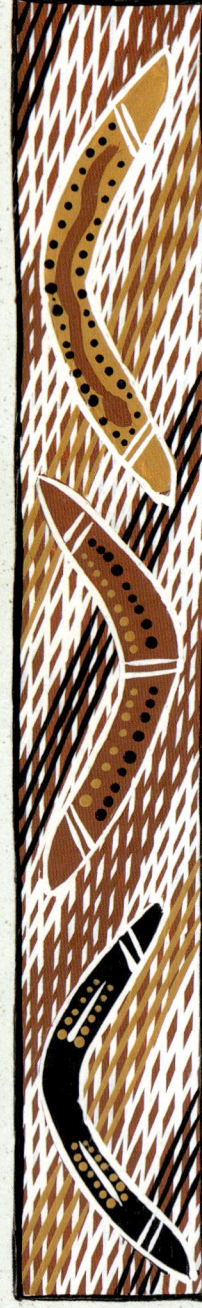

Hunters always tried to get as close as possible to the animal they were hunting before they threw a boomerang or spear at it.

Goose sticks

Bill Harney was a famous writer who lived with Aborigines in the Northern Territory for most of his life. He recorded the methods that Aboriginal hunters from the Finness River used to catch magpie geese. They climbed onto concealed platforms high up in bushy-topped paper-bark trees near lagoons on a flood-plain early in the morning. In the hair-belts around their waists they carried as many "goose sticks" as they could.

When a flock of magpie geese flew overhead, the hunters and other people hiding in bushes around the trees began to mimic the geese's call. Down came the flock of geese to join the birds that were calling to them. As soon as they flew close enough, they were showered with goose sticks, which knocked them wounded or unconscious to the ground. There, adults and children jumped on them and killed them before they could recover and fly away.

Magpie geese being barbecued.

Later, when the geese had been properly cooked over the coals, a story-teller of that clan told Bill Harney how one of their great creation ancestors, named Nemeuk, had taught them how to catch magpie geese that way.

These hunters did not need heavy hunting sticks, like the kind used to cripple kangaroos. They preferred light sticks that could be thrown up into a flock of geese flying overhead. The sticks had to be hard enough and heavy enough to knock the birds to the ground just long enough for the catchers to grab them.

Clubs and throwing sticks

Many throwing sticks have the familiar shape of the returning boomerang, but lack the special shape which sends them whirling back to the thrower. Some throwing sticks can be thrown so that they bounce up off the ground some distance in front of the thrower. These pick up speed and hit their target with great force. They can hit hard enough to cripple, stun and even kill the largest Australian animals and birds.

The boomerangs at the bottom of this picture lack the special shape which make them fly in a circle thereby returning to the thrower.

One particularly dangerous throwing stick had a hooked end or long beak. It was mainly used in fighting because it could hook onto a shield, swing around it and strike the person behind. Throwing sticks of this kind have been found from western Queensland, through central Australia and across to the Kimberleys in Western Australia. A very elaborately carved hooked boomerang was used in ceremonies in the Coopers Creek area in South Australia. In Victoria, Aborigines used similarly shaped carved sticks, called *leangles*, as clubs. They were also effective weapons for by-passing a shield.

A painted shield from Cairns.

These wooden clubs were used by Aborigines in Victoria.

Two other types of throwing sticks are also worth mentioning. *Lil-lils* were only made by Aborigines living in the upper reaches of the Murray River in Victoria. They are gracefully carved with a flat axe-like heads. The other type is a hunting boomerang generally made in the desert in the central west of Australia. It is called a *karlie* or *kaili*, which is sometimes spelled *kylie*, a popular girls' name these days.

A lil-lil from the Murray River.

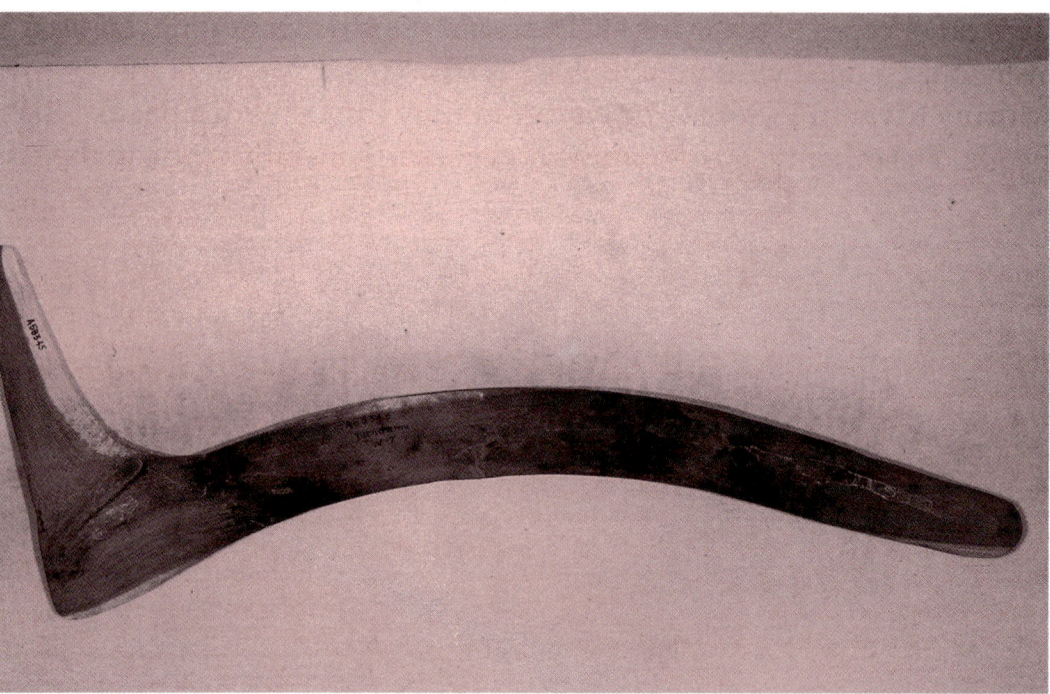

This "karlie" comes from Yuendumu in central Australia.

Although boomerangs and throwing sticks of a particular design, like that of the *lil-lil*, were only manufactured in the places where they originated, they were often traded over great distances. Hooked throwing sticks, for instance, were made in central and north-central Australia, but they have been found in Queensland and in Western Australia. The story of how goods were traded across Australia is a separate story in itself. Well-designed boomerangs and throwing sticks were always a popular trade item, especially since neither the techniques for carving them, nor the particular wood they were made from, were generally available throughout the country.

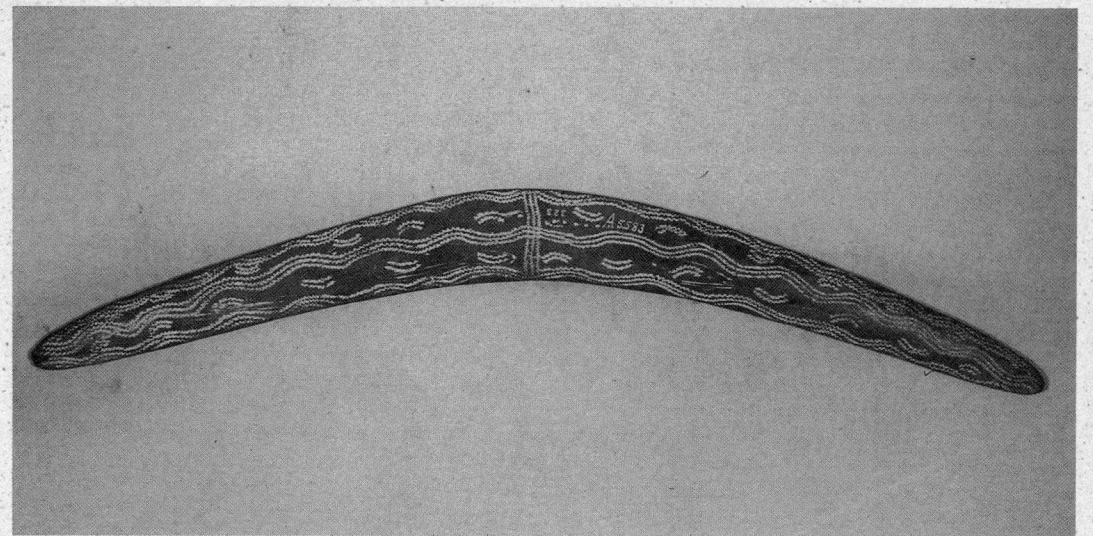

Many boomerangs featuring elaborately carved designs were traded for other items.

Aboriginal people usually designed their tools so that they could be used for a variety of purposes. A throwing stick could be thrown to bring down an emu; it could double as a digging stick; it could be rubbed on soft wood to make fire; it could have a sharp stone blade inserted in hard wax at one end to serve as a cutting tool or a scraper; and it could be used for tapping or clapping as an accompaniment to ceremonial music.

Aboriginal men and women had traditional obligations to their homelands which made it necessary for them to live and to seek food in different places according to the seasons. When they travelled they did not carry more tools and other **utensils** than they really needed. Having multipurpose tools made it easier to travel lightly over long distances, when such journeys were necessary.

In this ceremony, boomerangs are being used as musical instruments to beat time to the music.

Returning boomerangs

In its many shapes, the throwing stick has been a very important hunting, food-gathering, and fighting tool for Aboriginal people. For many of us the throwing-stick shape that is most familiar is that of the returning boomerang. It is often used as a **trademark** to identify Australian–made goods.

The shape of the returning boomerang also varies according to where it was made. Look at the boomerangs reproduced below. These are all genuine returning boomerangs, but notice how the angle of the arms varies as does the length of those arms and their width. These variations in design influence the way that they perform in the air. One would probably climb more steeply than the others. Another may swing in a wide flat curve rather than sweeping upwards. Some returning boomerangs are thrown so that they bounce up after hitting the ground.

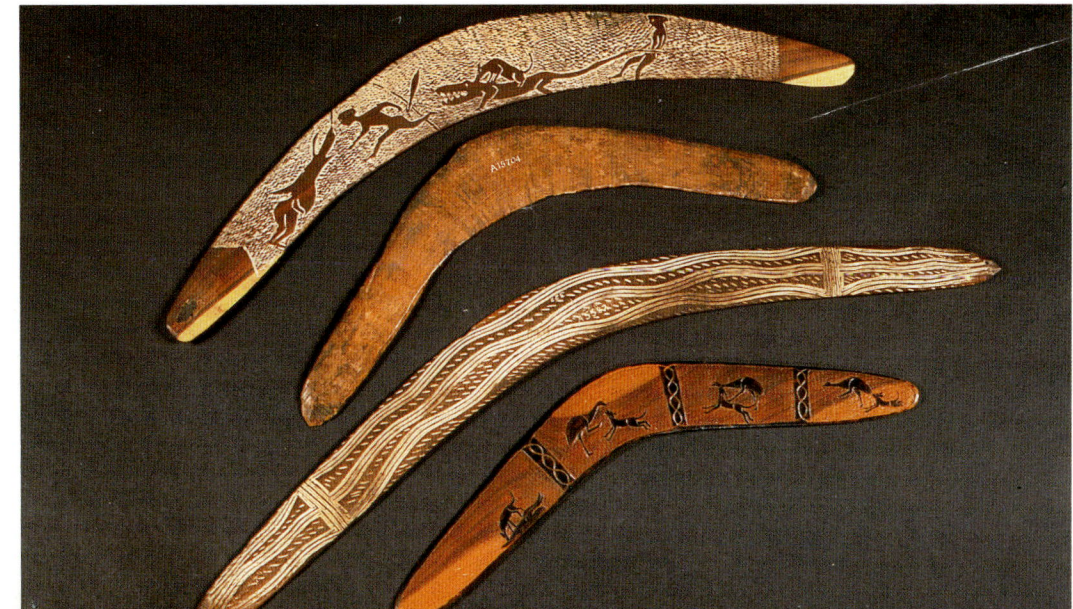

The design of the returning boomerang varies from region to region.

It takes a great deal of skill to send the boomerang into flight along the path the thrower wants it to take. Young boys will practise endlessly until the skill becomes automatic.

To throw a boomerang you must hold it at one end and lift it over and behind your shoulder with the ends of the arms pointing to the front. You then throw it forward into the air with a powerful twist of the wrist as it is released, to set it spinning. To increase the force of the throw, you can run a few paces forward, arch your back and twist your shoulders into the throw.

A boomerang may also be thrown downwards, horizontally or at an angle to the ground, depending on its shape and the flight path you want it to take. Because of its **aerodynamic** design, it will fly upwards on a curved flight path which, unless it accidentally hits something, will bring it back to the thrower. If thrown expertly it will return close enough to the thrower to be easily caught, or at least land nearby.

Modern boomerangs

This man is participating in a boomerang throwing competition.

Because throwing a boomerang to follow a set path and return to the hands of the thrower takes such great skill and practice, it is not surprising to find that boomerang throwing has become an international sport. In the United States of America there is a Boomerang Association and world championship boomerang throwing competitions have been held both there and in Australia.

Boomerangs thrown in these competitions are now made from many different materials, such as plastic and light-weight metal. New designs have improved their performance in the air, taking them further, longer and higher on their flight. However, they are still made using the same basic aerodynamic principles discovered by Aborigines.

Boomerangs can be bought which are made of plastic. The designs of these boomerangs have been copied from boomerangs which have been made for thousands of years.

If you get a chance, visit an Aboriginal arts and crafts centre and take a good look at the boomerangs made by Aborigines that they have on display. Apart from the decorations, which often distinguish where they were made and who made them, you should note that their design has changed little from that of the boomerangs in our museums that show us how they were made 20 000 years ago.

An Aboriginal arts and crafts shop.

Glossary

Aerodynamic The way in which an object has been designed to move through the air easily and smoothly.

Invention An entirely new apparatus or machine.

Peat Soil made from decomposed vegetable matter in marshy regions.

Trademark The symbol or word used by a manufacturer to distinguish his or her goods from those made by other manufacturers.

Utensils Any instrument or container commonly used in food preparation.

Index

A
American Indians 10

B
barragadan 7
birgan 7

C
clubs 13

D
digging sticks 11, 21

G
Georges River 7
goose sticks 15

H
Harney, Bill 15-16
hooked boomerangs 18

K
kaili 19

L
lil-lil 20

M
magpie geese 15, 16
Murray River 8
musical instruments 13

N
Nemeuk 16
New Hebrides 10

P
peat bog 11

R
returning boomerangs 8, 23

S
spears 13
stone tools 13

T
Tutankhamen 10

W
wonguin 7
wooden tools 11, 13
Wyrie Swamp 11-13

Reference

HARNEY, B. (1970) *Tales From the Aborigine*. Adelaide: Rigby (Seal).